IMPORTANT THINGS

poems by

Barbara L. Greenberg

Finishing Line Press
Georgetown, Kentucky

IMPORTANT THINGS

Copyright © 2018 by Barbara L. Greenberg
ISBN 978-1-63534-734-0 First Edition
All rights reserved under International and Pan-American Copyright Conventions. No part of this book may be reproduced in any manner whatsoever without written permission from the publisher, except in the case of brief quotations embodied in critical articles and reviews.

ACKNOWLEDGMENTS

"The Blind Boy" and "Food Stamps" and "Wolfprints" were published in *Northwest Review*
"Important Things" was published in *The Iowa Review*, anthologized in *Sudden Fiction: American Short-Stories* (Peregrine Smith Books) and was quoted in its entirety by R.V. Cassill in the 4th edition of *The North Anthology of Short Fiction*
"The Princess" was published by *The Bradley Broadside*
"The First Kiss" was published by *Pieces*

Publisher: Leah Maines
Editor: Christen Kincaid
Cover Art: Nathan Greenberg
Author Photo: Vicky Kabadikoni
Cover Design: Elizabeth Maines McCleavy

Printed in the USA on acid-free paper.
Order online: www.finishinglinepress.com
 also available on amazon.com

Author inquiries and mail orders:
Finishing Line Press
P. O. Box 1626
Georgetown, Kentucky 40324
U. S. A.

Table of Contents

Important Things 1

Dog Years 3

Wolfprints 4

Princess 5

Enough Already 7

Twins 8

The Blind Boy 10

The Quiet Girl 12

First Kiss 13

A Cold Person 15

Occupied 17

Hell No 18

You 20

*For
Nathan M. Greenberg
and
Leslie Lawrence
Fondly and appreciativly*

IMPORTANT THINGS

For years the children whimpered and tugged. "Tell us, tell us."

You promised to tell the children some other time, later, when they were old enough.

Now the children stand eye to eye with you and show you their teeth. "Tell us."

"Tell you what?" you ask, ingenuous.

"Tell us The Important Things."

You tell your children there are six continents and five oceans, or vice versa.

You tell your children the little you know about sex. Your children tell you there are better words for what you choose to call The Married Embrace.

You tell your children to be true to themselves. They say they are true to themselves. You tell them they're lying, you always know when they're lying. They tell you you're crazy. You tell them to mind their manners. They think you mean it as a joke. They laugh.

There are tears in your eyes. You tell the children the dawn will follow the dark, the tide will come in, the grass will be renewed, every dog will have its day. You tell them the story of the Littlest Soldier whose right arm, which he sacrificed while fighting for a noble cause, grew back again.

You say that if there were no Evil we wouldn't have the satisfaction of choosing The Good. And if there were no pain, you say, we'd never know our greatest joy, relief from pain.

You offer to bake a cake for the children, a fudge cake with chocolate frosting, their favorite.

"Tell us," say the children.

You say to your children, "I am going to die."

"When?"

"Someday."

"Oh."

You tell your children that they, too, are going to die. They already knew it.

You can't think of anything else to tell the children. You say you're sorry. You are sorry. But the children have had enough of your excuses.

"A promise is a promise," say the children.

They'll give you one more chance to tell them of your own accord. If you don't, they have to resort to torture.

DOG YEARS

It wasn't a surprise. Your mom and dad explained that the dog was old and getting ready to die. Parents who share their home with a dog are aware that it's likely to die before they do. That's one of the reasons. They tell their children that dog years are different from human years. Whether dog years are shorter than human years, or longer but fewer, you still aren't certain, but you got the point.

Dogs are God's way of teaching little children about Life and Death and how they fit together like day and night. How an ant is not so different from the president of the USA. People give dogs names like Spot and Rover and Lassie but a better name for any dog is Mort. The word mortality can be introduced later. Dogs and cats and grandparents and caged birds – they disappear. Here one day and gone the next, as people say.

Remember when little you lay flat on the floor of the back seat of your daddy's car and disappeared yourself? The police came, and all the neighbors. You heard your name being called by many voices. They were afraid you'd been stolen. Or had died. After hours of hiding on the floor of the car and everyone thinking you'd died or been stolen, you thought so too. Eventually you fell asleep. Next morning you woke up in your own bed, wondering how you got there. You called out the name of your dog, not expecting an answer.

Yes, it was your fault that the dog died. God punishes naughty little boys and girls by taking away something they really love. You really loved that dog and that dog loved you back. Even when you pulled its tail and twisted its ears, your old dog understood that you were just a child and didn't bite you.

WOLFPRINTS

The others have not been keeping a record of the times you didn't ask for anything, the times you didn't cry for help or beg be admitted.

These times are likely to your credit, but you alone can give yourself credit. If ever you should ask for anything or cry for help or beg to be admitted, if ever you should speak, you'll face a blind statistical risk of interrupting, introducing complications, forcing out a yes or a no, producing awkwardness, inciting trouble.

You were taught that to cry wolf is the greatest shame of all. You were taught that the person who cries wolf today will be eaten by the wolf tomorrow. Each time the possibility of the wolf appears, you let it come within an inch of you. You meet its eyes, you verify its teeth, you sniff its breath for signs of wolfishness. You don't cry wolf, you never have. Afterwards, you're always glad you didn't.

No one other than you yourself can give you credit for the times you didn't, but your record of those times is incomplete. You have no data on the times you didn't. You were led to believe there would be a Record Keeper but there is no Record Keeper. All that's left is your own imperfect record.

Oh, but look! Something akin to rain has happened here—the ink has bled and faded. Of the innumerable times you didn't nothing remains but smudges.

At the end of your story is the locked door. You journey to this door and ask for Everything. Through the transom comes a voice explaining what you might have done each time you didn't. This voice describes the sights you could have seen if you had not, for fear of introducing complications, covered your face at consummating moments. This pickax of a voice is saying everything except Come in.

You speak to it.

You beg to be admitted.

THE PRINCESS

As soon as she'd learned to walk and speak, they secured her with a harness and a length of rope to a strong tethering tree.

Between this little princess and the one you used to be there is not a hair of difference. "Look at our little princess in her new pink frock," her mother said. Surely you remember your mother saying that about you.

And your father the tailor, who was just then knotting the final stitch on your harness, said in return, "Indeed she is a little princess. We must keep her safe, clean and happy."

Your house was on a high bluff overlooking a violent sea. The tree was a stout willow with iron roots. The rope was long, life long. Over the years it might wear to less than a thread, to scarcely more than a thin melodic line spun on a violin—but it was never going to snap, no risk of that.

You toddled to the edge of the bluff and watched for shipwreck.

"Other families have babysitters," said your mother to your father. "Some families have nannies and governesses. I myself would hold my head up higher if we could afford something human."

"Human nature is a snake in the grass," your father said.

Harnessed and pinafored you went to school. Harnessed and furred you travelled abroad. When they summoned you home to the castle keep, you were still harnessed.

"When is our LP coming down for dinner?"

"Not tonight, my dear. She is eating alone. Our princess is a vegetarian now. Her flesh and blood disgust her."

"So be it, my dear. Be glad she is not off marching in the Renaissance."

Is the moon full? Indeed, it is splendidly full. Secure on your tether, you lower yourself from your bedroom window and run to the edge of the bluff. There, like a tall ship's figurehead, you lean out over the moonwashed sea.

A prince emerges from a smashed wave, pulls himself up onto a rock, holds out his arms for you: "Come down!"

"Climb up," you call back, not seeing his chains.

And thus it continues and echoes: "Come down!" "Climb up!"

ENOUGH ALREADY

A bowl of candy kisses was your nemesis. They gave you one. You asked for two. Shame on you for wanting two, they told you. But two was never really what you wanted. You wanted two times two times two times everything.

There is plenty of good food. Always, at the center of your table, there is a bowl of fruit. Pears and apples, apples and pears, most plentiful. But these apples have taught you nothing. These pears give no milk.

They said your eyes were bigger than your stomach. Behind your eyes you grew another pair of eyes, voracious squids. With those unseeing eyes you ate them out of house and home the way they said you would.

You meant it when you thanked them when they locked you in. Better the prison of home than freedom in the dark brown forest of your appetite. You'd been there once upon a time; you knew the plot. When you were Hansel/Gretel you ate an entire house, down to the last sweet brick of it. Then you ate the roasted witch—head, feet and all. You ate the witch the way you ate the house: *chomp chomp chomp chomp.* After all that eating, you were still hungry.

There is plenty of good food. The farmers are waltzing. The grapes are like plums, the plums are like melons, the melons are like pigs, the pigs are like hippopotami. No one anywhere on earth is suffering for lack of that which you are about to eat.

Bon appetit!

TWINS

Twin is depressed: sick of soul, muscles aching, out of love, out of steam. You understand. You've served some time yourself. What Twin needs is a shot of air.

"Come on, Twin. Let's go for a walk."

(Twin doesn't say no.)

You walk Twin down Dolphin Road, which leads to the river. Oh what a day this is, a new spring day, so much to see! "Look, Twin: grass, shrubs, kids, cars, dogs, trees, birds, roofs, clouds..." But Twin is shuttered off, so Twin can't see.

At the bottom of Dolphin you say to Twin, "Let's cross here and walk by the river."

Twin tells you that walking is out of the question. Can't walk. Never learned how.

There isn't any traffic, so you cross. Twin doesn't follow. You cross back and take Twin by the hand. You pull and pull at Twin, whose legs don't budge.

"Now look what you've done!"

You don't know what you've done, but you're sincerely sorry. You'll be a cane for Twin. You're strong, you'll carry Twin. Or else you'll call a cab. An ambulance? Twin needs this help you badly need to give.

Twin says you've helped enough, too much, already.

You hear yourself saying goodbye. You start to go.

(Twin doesn't say don't go.)

So here you are alone on a bench facing the river, not seeing the river, not hearing it either, not hearing anything except the footsteps which are not Twin's footsteps on the path behind you…

Until they are! Here's Twin, walking toward you. You can't contain yourself, you fling yourself at Twin…

"Hooray! You walked, I knew you could!"

And Twin says "I did not."

And you say "But…"

And Twin says "You! You spoil everything!"

THE BLIND BOY

What a curious predicament. Wherever you go these days a blind boy goes with you, singing his little songs, chanting his questions. "What are you doing? What are you doing now? Now what are you doing?"

The blind boy, who sees nothing, imagines everything.

There's no use trying to hide from the blind boy. In any combat of the senses, this child has you beaten four to one.

Today you're talking tough to the blind boy, hoping he'll learn to despise you.

"Get lost, little boy."

"But I am lost."

"What about your dog, shouldn't you have a dog?"

The blind boy doesn't have a dog. He doesn't even have a cat, he says. "But I have you," says the blind boy, smiling. For a smile that's never seen a mirror, it's a pretty nice smile.

You tell the blind boy you're sorry the feeling isn't mutual. You tell him he's a pest. You tell him you're a busy person with important work to do and others on your conscience so you don't need him.

"Couldn't I maybe rub your feet?" the blind boy says.

You take a dollar from your wallet and put it in the blind boy's pocket. You say you wish it could be more but you've already made your annual contribution to the Helen Keller Fund.

"Thank you," says the blind boy. "You are the soul of generosity. I am proud to have you as my only friend."

Poor you, powerless against the blind boy's powerlessness. You need a different strategy.

"Tell me where you live, and I'll walk you home."

"I live in the dark," he says. "What about you?"

Can you admit to the blind boy that you, too, live in the dark?

"I live in the real world," you say.

The blind boy laughs and takes you by the hand.

"Let's go."

THE QUIET GIRL

You remember the quiet girl, the one you were always listening for, the one who kept her head cocked as if she herself were listening for God knows what, you never asked, she never said.

Yes, that quiet girl, the one you almost spoke to.

When the quiet girl left the building, early and alone, you thought of following her. You thought of asking her to show you her scars. You felt she would, you were afraid she would. You turned to follow her and then turned back.

What became of the quiet girl? She was the one everybody lost track of, the one they never stop asking about. "Remember her? What ever happened to her?"

Sometimes, in crowds, you notice a girl with a disturbing expression on her face, and you feel a sudden cramp in your heart. You wonder what the connection could be, not realizing that the connection is the quiet girl.

She lived in a brown three-decker, not far from where you used to live. The next time your find yourself in the old neighborhood, you are going to drive around and around until you locate that house. Then you are going to park outside and wait. Maybe a door will be opened. Maybe the quiet girl will come out singing.

THE FIRST KISS

Until you and s/he have reached an understanding about the first kiss, a second kiss, you say, is quite unthinkable.

The birdsong must be accounted for. Also the marmalade.

The story line, you say, is unacceptably ambiguous. It is not yet known whether s/he premeditated the first kiss, or whether you did, or whether the first kiss was in fact spontaneous. And how can one proceed without a working definition of spontaneity?

The qualities of the first kiss are thus far undefined, you say. Lip-connected variables have yet to be agreed upon and isolated. Questions of texture, questions of pressure and flexibility, questions relating to prior use and health and shelf life remain unanswered.

S/he apologizes for having experienced the first kiss artlessly. S/he offers to repeat the first kiss with a heightened consciousness.

"No soap," you say.

You wonder whether the first kiss should be framed like the first dollar or bronzed like the first baby shoes. S/he tells you to consult your mom; you see the point. Still, you defend your mother's coffee-table values and your mother's kisses.

"Is this an argument?" s/he asks.

You say you guess it is.

"Let's kiss and make up," s/he says, which is out of the question. The question is custody, the custody of the first kiss. You mean to fight for it. S/he means to let you have your half without a fight. Stricken, you roll your eyes and sink to your knees.

"King Solomon," you cry, "better that s/he possess the first kiss intact than it be split in two and surely perish."

Oh you are subtle and sly; you establish your claim. Whipped and abashed, s/he defers to your claim, signing away all rights to the first kiss. Even the right of visitation? Yes.

S/he is leaving down. Without a word to you s/he is out the door. You go to the window and watch as s/he crosses the street: a sorry, wind-blown figure in a sad, brown coat. A harder heart than yours would break at the sight.

"Come back," you shout from the window. "Come back, come back."

S/he does come back. And now you enter into the long, slow, painful process of the second kiss.

A COLD PERSON

First they wound you cruelly. Then they rush to your aid: "Are you hurt, are you hurt?" They're already ready to bury the hatchet, to kiss and be kissed and pass the pipe around.

That's when you give them the cold shoulder, proving that you are indeed the kind of person they'd always said you were.

Cold people are known by their eyes, by their cold eyes. Your eyes are icy blue or arctic green. Those are the choices.

The "brown" that's written on your driver's license and on your retina is irrelevant now. Stories about your glacial stare turning colleagues to ice are not to be taken literally, but neither are they to be taken lightly.

A cold person cannot enter a room without looking and smelling like frost.

"Good morning," you say. "Nice weather we're having." Say what you will, there'll be an ill wind blowing. All words are serpents' teeth in the mouth of a cold person.

When people with bruises head to toe claim to have gotten those bruises in your bed, they'll be believed. Then when you say you sleep alone, you've always slept alone, they'll cry out "Gotcha!" Cold people are their own worst evidence.

There are times you want to shout at them: *I am not, I am not cold!* Other times you wish you were, you think you'll try to be. Some winter night when the others imagine you alone in your stark white room still entertaining yourself with the little blizzard inside that glass globe paperweight you've always liked to play with, they'll be wrong, dead wrong. You will have run away. You will have changed your name to something insouciant, something like Sang Froid. Oh the avalanches you'll survive, the peaks you'll scale, the ice-locked palaces you'll have your visions in! And oh the Bipolar Symphony you'll compose by the light of the Aurora

Borealis, for which you'll be acclaimed world-wide! Putative lovers will boast that certain marks on your body were made by you in the heat of your passion.

This too will run its course. Then they'll begin to know you as the kind of person that in fact you are, you think.

OCCUPIED

You want not to be heard, not to be interrupted. Not to be witnessed, not to be prevented, not ever to be reminded.

You stare at the ceiling. The minute you notice a spider on the ceiling, you focus on it. You watch the spider lower itself on a filament, descending faster than you thought a spider could. Is the spider about to settle on your face? Can you endure the feeling of spider-on-your-face without crying out?

But when the spider comes within an inch above your nose, it stops. It simply hangs, immobile, huge in your vision. It is a gray, hairy spider, very fat.

"Hello, Mother," you say.

HELL NO!

You seldom knew where you were until you were told.

"What? Hell? This place is Hell? I should have seen the sign? What sign? Oh yes, that sign. But look, look—some joker has added an o to it."

So for a long time you couldn't get your bearings. Your knees buckled and your vision blurred. Arrows that others understood to be pointing straight ahead seemed to you to be pointing skyward. It was said of you that your head was in the clouds and that those lazy feet of yours were not planted firm on the ground.

So much for living on a higher plane! Tired of being neither here nor there, you took the conventional route and consulted a doctor.

"I'm at the wrong altitude," you said to her.

"Attitude is important," she replied. "With the right attitude, mountains can be moved."

"Doctor, I walk on air!"

"Walking on a hair is difficult. Still, we all tread a fine line these days."

"On air," you persisted, exhaling for emphasis. "There's a layer of air between me and the surface. As with a hydrofoil."

"A side of oil? That's most unusual. And yet you're constipated?"

"A hydrofoil. A boat."

"Aha, bloat. Quite consistent with the rest of your symptoms.

The bloat-float syndrome, we in the profession call it. The magic word is roughage. Roughage, my dear."

The doctor was correct. It was roughage that brought you down. Its source was an old man with a cane, a very old man whose shopping bag was obviously too heavy for him, a superannuated man alongside whom you were about to cross a busy street.

"Let me help you with your bundle" is what you said to him.

"No thank you," said he.

"Please. The weight of it will give me my footing."

"No thank you. No."

"Sir," you said, your voice roughening, closing in on him, "you don't understand. I am in dire need of ballast. I insist you let me carry your bag."

"Help, help," the old man cried, and shook his cane at you but being infirm he couldn't prevent you from seizing his bag and fleeing the scene like the criminal you had just become.

From that day on everything changed in you. As you consumed the old man's groceries you gained your bearings, your footing, your equilibrium, and a sense of your own tainted humanity.

Now when you dream about the old man crossing the street, he isn't calling for help. Sometimes what he is saying is "To hell with you." Other times: "Hello!"

YOU

    Although others may think of you as self-assured and cheerful, your nature, like the moon, has a dark side to it. However assertive you seem, you are basically shy.

    Persons born under your sign experience conflict. They are no strangers to the pitch and roll of longing.

    Your capacity for love is never wholly realized. You harbor feelings for which there are no right words. Sometimes, when you consider the mysteries of Life on Earth, your time here seems little more than a passing cloud.

    There is something close to devoutness in your nature. However many dogmas you renounce, you never lose your innate instinct for prayer.

    Two is one of your lucky numbers.

    Among your favorite colors is the color blue.

Barbara **(Levenson) Greenberg** is the author of *The Spoils of August* (1974), *The Never-not Sonnets* (1989), *What Nell Knows* (1997), *Fire Drills: Stories* (1982) and *Late Life Happiness* (2010). She has taught poetry and prose writing at several Boston area colleges and was an originating faculty member of the MFA writing programs at Goddard and Warren Wilson colleges. In 1999 she was appointed a scholar at Brandeis Women's Studies Research Center.

Barbara L. Greenberg was graduated from Wellesley College in 1953 and received a master's degree from Simmons a decade later. In 1955 she married the late Harold L. Greenberg, a distinguished surgeon, raised two sons and currently delights in the company of her grandchildren, Nathan and Rebecca.

www.ingramcontent.com/pod-product-compliance
Lightning Source LLC
LaVergne TN
LVHW040118080426
835507LV00041B/1786